Fangs and Teeth

Written by Brylee Gibson

Fangs and Teeth

Most animals have teeth.
In some animals the teeth are called fangs.
Fangs and teeth can be very sharp.
Animals use them to hunt and eat food.
Some animals can grow new teeth,
and others have teeth in different places.

tarantula

Komodo dragons

pit viper

viperfish

cookie-cutter shark

3

A spider has two jaws.
Inside these jaws are big fangs.
The spider uses these fangs to stab its prey.
Some spiders can swing their fangs
into their prey like an axe.
Other spiders use their fangs
to pinch their prey.

tarantula

the fangs move
up and down

huntsman spider

the fangs move
in and out

The viper snake is another animal with fangs.
The fangs are very long and very sharp.
They are so sharp, they can stab through
an animal's fur and feathers.
When the viper is not using its fangs,
it can fold them back inside its mouth.
No other snake can do this!

pit viper

fangs swing out

fangs

A viper can fold its fangs into its mouth and swing them out when it bites an animal.

dolphin

... a hole left by the cookie-cutter shark

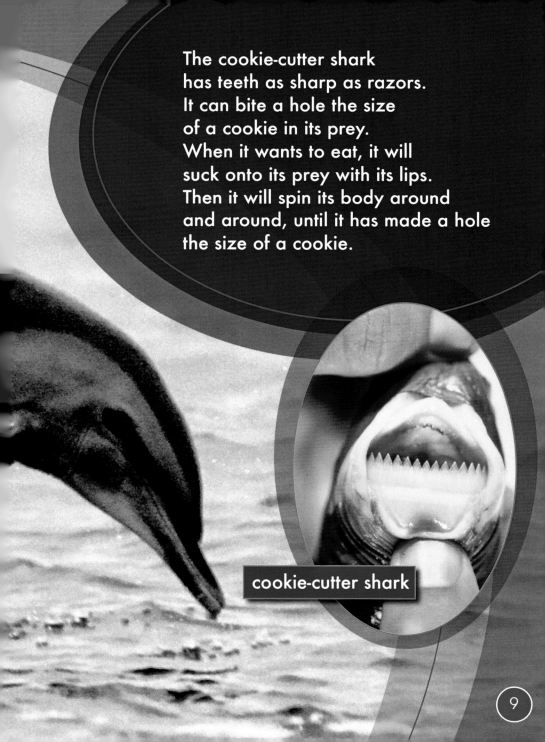

The cookie-cutter shark
has teeth as sharp as razors.
It can bite a hole the size
of a cookie in its prey.
When it wants to eat, it will
suck onto its prey with its lips.
Then it will spin its body around
and around, until it has made a hole
the size of a cookie.

cookie-cutter shark

Komodo dragon

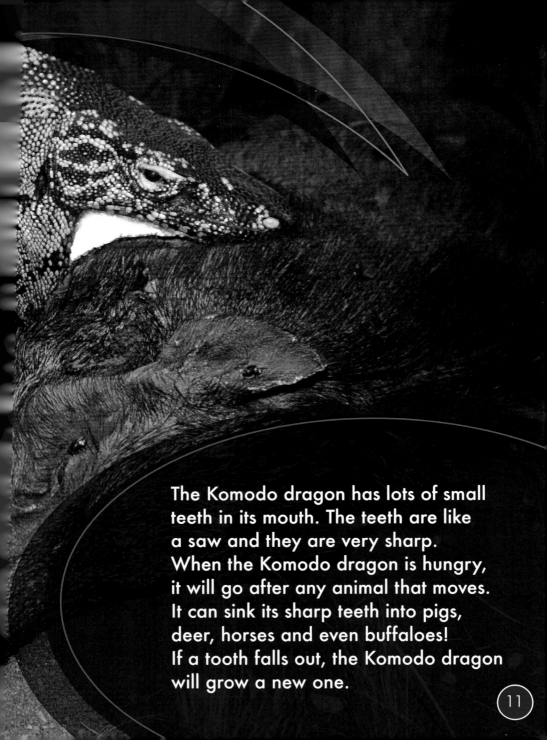

The Komodo dragon has lots of small
teeth in its mouth. The teeth are like
a saw and they are very sharp.
When the Komodo dragon is hungry,
it will go after any animal that moves.
It can sink its sharp teeth into pigs,
deer, horses and even buffaloes!
If a tooth falls out, the Komodo dragon
will grow a new one.

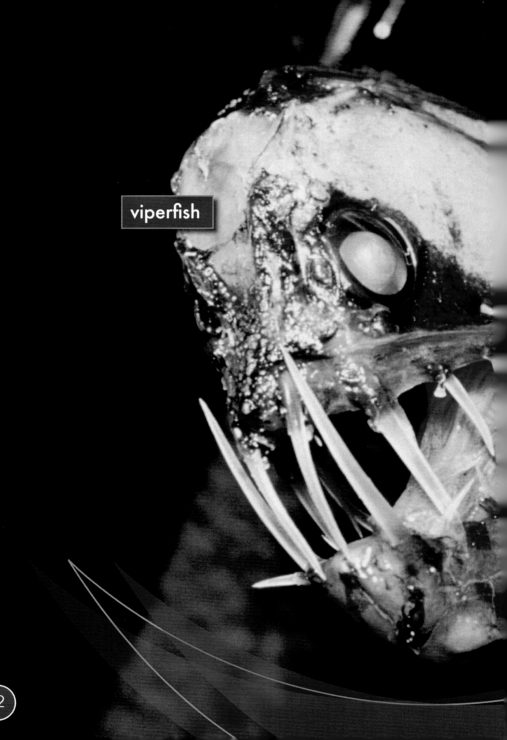

viperfish

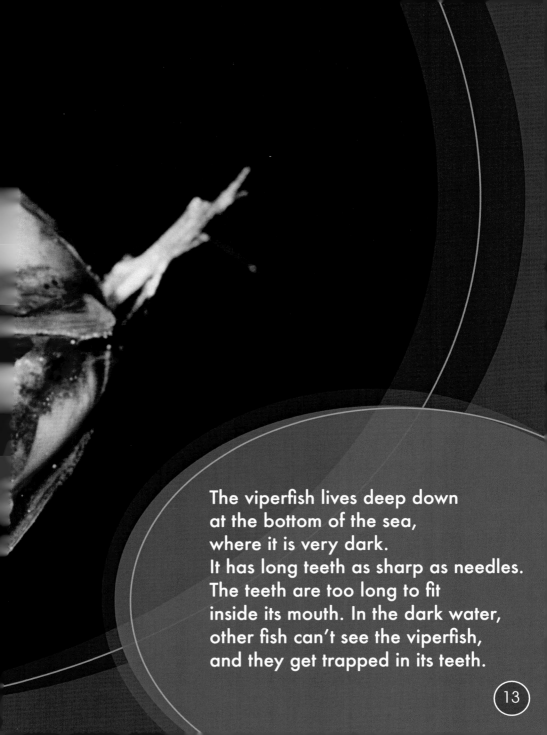

The viperfish lives deep down
at the bottom of the sea,
where it is very dark.
It has long teeth as sharp as needles.
The teeth are too long to fit
inside its mouth. In the dark water,
other fish can't see the viperfish,
and they get trapped in its teeth.

A goldfish does not have any teeth
inside its mouth at all.
But it has some tiny, sharp teeth
inside its throat!
It uses these teeth to crush up food
before the food gets to its stomach.

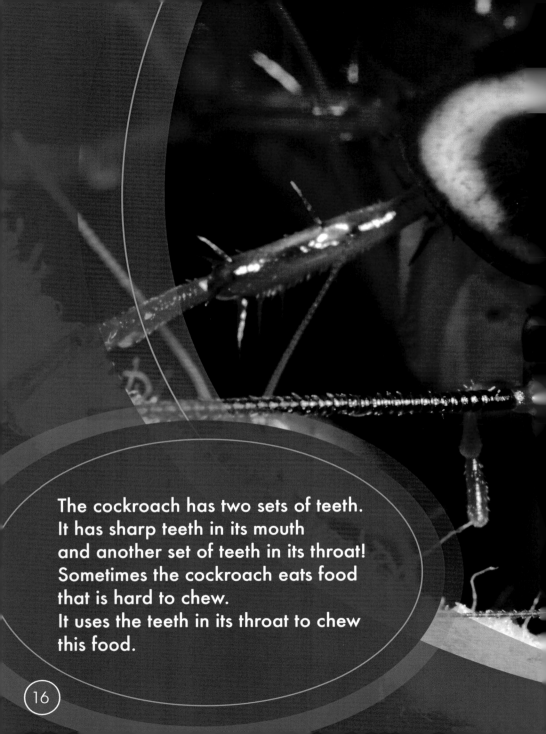

The cockroach has two sets of teeth.
It has sharp teeth in its mouth
and another set of teeth in its throat!
Sometimes the cockroach eats food
that is hard to chew.
It uses the teeth in its throat to chew
this food.

Spiders have fangs to stab their prey.

Vipers have fangs that can fold back inside their mouth.

The Komodo dragon has lots of small, sharp teeth.

Fangs and Teeth

A goldfish has tiny, sharp teeth in its throat to crush up food.

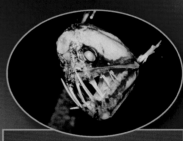

The viperfish has very long, sharp teeth that stick out of its mouth.

Index

The cookie-cutter shark has sharp teeth that bite holes in its prey.

fangs
      spider 4
      viper snake 6

teeth
      cockroach 16
      cookie-cutter shark 9
      goldfish 14
      Komodo dragon 11
      viperfish 13

A cockroach has two sets of teeth. One set of teeth is in its mouth and the other set is in its throat.

Guide Notes

Title: Fangs and Teeth
Stage: Launching Fluency – Orange

Genre: Non-fiction
Approach: Guided Reading
Processes: Thinking Critically, Exploring Language, Processing Information
Written and Visual Focus: Illustrative Diagrams, Labels, Captions, Index
Word Count: 381

THINKING CRITICALLY

(sample questions)
- What do you know about fangs and teeth on animals?
- What might you expect to see in this book?
- Look at the index. Encourage the students to think about the information and make predictions about the text content.
- Look at pages 4 and 5. What do you think is meant by the words *swing their fangs into their prey like an axe*?
- Look at pages 6 and 7. Why do you think the viper's fangs need to be so sharp?
- Look at pages 8 and 9. How do you know that the cookie-cutter shark's teeth are as sharp as razors?
- Look at pages 10 and 11. What might cause the Komodo dragon's tooth to fall out?
- What things in the book have helped you to understand the information?
- What questions do you have after reading the text?

EXPLORING LANGUAGE

Terminology
Photograph credits, index

Vocabulary
Clarify: fangs, razors, prey
Singular/Plural: animal/animals, jaw/jaws, feather/feathers, pig/pigs
Homonyms: saw/sore, prey/pray, one/won, new/knew

Print Conventions
Apostrophes – possessive (animal's), contraction (can't)